You Know You're a
Cricket Fanatic
When...

Mike Haskins
& Clive Whichelow

summersdale

YOU KNOW YOU'RE A CRICKET FANATIC WHEN…

Summersdale Publishers Ltd
46 West Street
Chichester
West Sussex
PO19 1RP
UK

www.summersdale.com

Printed and bound in China

ISBN: 978-1-84953-048-4

Substantial discounts on bulk quantities of Summersdale books are available to corporations, professional associations and other organisations. For details contact Summersdale Publishers by telephone: +44 (0) 1243771107, fax: +44 (0) 1243 786300 or email: nicky@summersdale.com.

You Know You're a
Cricket Fanatic
When...

You shout 'howzat!' every time you catch a bus.

You plan your wedding round the
Test series.

You wonder why people look surprised when you tell them you like nothing better than sitting on your own for hours oiling your bat.

Your favourite holiday destinations are Australia, the West Indies, New Zealand, Pakistan, and, er, Headingley.

You think a test tube is a train to
the Oval.

You claim your favourite movies are
The Umpire Strikes Back and
The Wicket Man.

A child points to a 'dickie bird' and you expect to see a man in a white coat.

You won't let your family use the phone
while the Test match is on in case your
team needs to call you for advice.

You wear white clothes at all times –
even to funerals.

Your favourite songs are 'Howzat', 'Bat Out of Hell', 'Fielder Beat', 'Ashes to Ashes' and 'I'm Spinning Around'.

You have Richie Benaud's voice on your satnav.

Your friends are beginning to dread your cricket-themed parties.

Your partner has got tired of you
calling them 'a great catch'.

Every time you see a man with a wooden leg, you have an overwhelming urge to throw a ball at him.

Every pair of trousers you own has a
red streaky patch down one leg.

You end all phone calls with
'over and out'.

Your favourite bands are the Spin Doctors, Bowling for Soup and, of course, Buddy Holly and the Crickets.

You are the only one doing overarm throws at the ten-pin bowling alley.

You once got thrown out of a
restaurant for meatball tampering.

You have spent significant amounts of time trying to find a hairdresser still prepared to give you a 1980s Ian Botham-style tinted mullet and 'tache.

You always eat curry before a match so
you're guaranteed to get the runs.

Your only clothes that aren't white
are your brightly coloured pyjamas,
which you refer to as your 'one-day
international kit'.

Your wife asks you to throw her the car keys and you can't resist putting a bit of a spin on them.

You thought the 'South African Boycott' of the 1970s was a black cricket player.

At your wedding the bride was in white and the groom was in... white (with a few grass stains).

You include your batting average on your CV.

You even named your daughters after cricketers – which would have been all right if you'd called them Viv, Grace, Dolly and Vera, but not Beefy, Freddy, Gooch and Ramprakash.

You have broken off from one or more of the following activities to check the Test score: having sex; attending a family funeral; the birth of your child; rescuing someone from a burning building.

You always manage to misunderstand
the dustmen at Christmas and end up
giving them a cricket box.

You have only ever owned two pets:
a cricket and a bat.

You always have Shredded Wheat for breakfast because it's the only cereal Ian Botham ever advertised.

You always reply in pitch lengths when
asked for directions.

You get your children to behave by threatening to make them listen to a detailed explanation of the LBW rule if they don't.

You decide to paint your living room yellow to match all the copies of *Wisden* on your shelves.

Taking up running didn't make you any
fitter because each time you went out
you only did 22 yards.

You have injured yourself more than once as a result of using a mallet to test the resistance of your new cricket box whilst you were wearing it.

You watched an entire *Batman* film before realising it wasn't going to include any cricket.

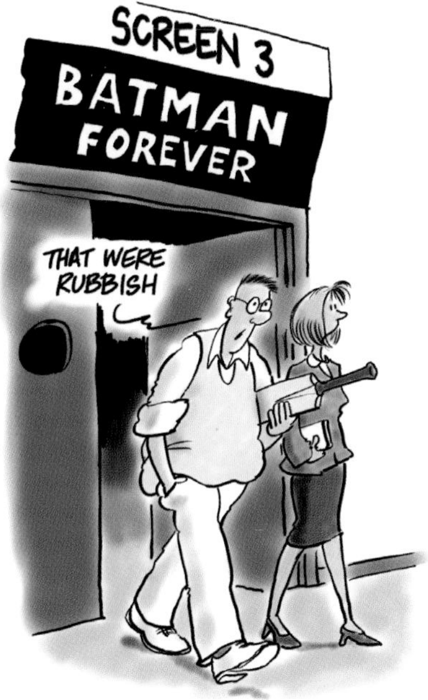
SCREEN 3
BATMAN FOREVER
THAT WERE RUBBISH

You get confused when someone recently departed is said to have had 'a good innings'.

You insisted on being surrounded by white reflective screens for any hospital operation you have.

Bowling a maiden over only has one meaning in your vocabulary.

You have a pavilion built on the back of your house instead of a conservatory.

Your office doors are marked 'out' and 'not out'.

You grow a bushy Merv Hughes moustache but are disappointed when none of the men who follow you home turn out to be cricket fans.

You always opt for the one-stripe-across-the-nose-and-cheeks Adam Ant look when applying sun cream.

You go out wearing your wicket keeper's gloves to keep warm in winter.

You ask to be cremated abroad so you can ensure the ashes will come back home.

You can't understand why you put weight on when you only drink as much as the members of your national team – and, if anything, you get more exercise than they do.

You buy your youngest child full-size pads, even though just one of them completely obscures his entire body.

Your partner is kept awake each night by you muttering historic Test scores in your sleep.

You know several hundred obscene expressions all synonymous with the term 'butterfingers'.

You have told your children that, when playing an over in the back garden, concussing one of the neighbours counts as a six.

You are confused to hear that there is an international 'No ball' prize.

Your doctor checks your heartbeat and hears the opening bars of 'Soul Limbo' by Booker T and the MGs.

You refuse to eat duck on principle.

You position your bed 22 yards from your bathroom so if you have to run to the toilet in the night you look on it as a practice session.

You always see a hailstorm as a golden
opportunity to hone your
catching skills.

You think a Dutch cap is a European cricket award.

You have a life-size model of W. G. Grace in your downstairs toilet.

You have used any of the following as improvised cricket equipment: a 12-inch ruler and a scrunched up piece of paper; a French loaf and a bread roll; a frying pan and a hard-boiled egg; a garden spade and a turnip.

You are disappointed to find that
you had misread the local amateur
dramatic society's poster and they
aren't putting on *Crease – The Musical*
after all.

You look down your nose at any sporting activities that take less than five days.

You rate looks, common interests, sense of humour and sexual compatibility as less important attributes than the ability to make teas when looking for your ideal partner.

You have to concentrate when polishing a shiny red apple in case you absent-mindedly go on to throw it at the nearest passer-by.

You lull yourself to sleep each night
by counting your least-favourite team
scoring runs.

Your favourite rap artist is
MCC Hammer.

Your national team selectors have had to change their phone numbers after you managed to get hold of them.

Every time you're in a field you automatically spend half an hour watching it before you realise there isn't a match going on.

You are shocked to find that sledging
is an Olympic sport.

Many people think you must be a religious fundamentalist because you revere a bearded man who lived long ago and hold an ancient text as sacred – except in your case it's W. G. Grace and the *Wisden Cricketers' Almanack*.

You take all your holidays from
Thursday to the following Tuesday.

You regularly book yourself onto your local open-top bus sightseeing tour so you can pretend you're doing a victory parade.

You measure your age in overs – apart from your half-century, of course.

Have you enjoyed this book?
If so, why not write a review
on your favourite website?

Thanks very much for buying
this Summersdale book.

www.summersdale.com